The Sorcerer's Arc

June English

Hearing Eye

Published by Hearing Eye 2004

Hearing Eye
Box 1, 99 Torriano Avenue
London NW5 2RX, UK
email: hearing_eye@torriano.org
www.torriano.org

ISBN: 1870841 09 3

Acknowledgements
Thanks are due the following magazines in which some of these poems first
appeared: Acumen, Brittle Star, Connections, Envoi, Equinox, Frogmore Papers,
Iota, Mslexia, Orbis, Outposts, Poetry Digest, Psychopoetica, The South and
Thanet User Forum 9FURSTO.

Five of the poems in this book first appeared in a pamphlet
Counting the Spots, (Acumen Publications 2000).

This publication has been made possible with
the financial support of Arts Council England

Printed by Catford Print Centre

Designed by Martin Parker at silbercow.co.uk   Cover illustration by Emily Johns

Contents

Introduction

There are two things I particularly like about the poetry of June English. The first is that her poems are not much like anyone else's. Of course that might not be a recommendation in every case, for bad poetry can be very distinctive in its badness. But no, June English is not like that at all, she's good, she's very good, assured, skilful and, particularly in the poems she has written in the last two years or so, very much herself, with her own voice, idiosyncratic, cranky even and isn't much of the best poetry cranky? Think of Blake, Emily Dickinson, Stevie Smith, Philip Larkin. I think of all these people (not all at once of course) when I think of June English. A new poem from her prompts in me the happy response 'I wonder what she's done this time.'

The other thing I like about her poetry is its range. She can be funny, vulgar, knowledgeable, pedantic, plain-spoken, equivocal, shocking (yes, really) and very, very sad. About the only thing she can't do is to write poems you can't make head nor tail of – but we all know that, alas, there's no shortage of that sort of thing. So let us be grateful for what we have got – a poet rooted here in East Kent, but not 'local' in the minimalising, patronising sense, who will speak to everyone, everywhere. This is a splendid book.

John Whitworth

The Tree That Isn't There

Once I slept through a hurricane
that uprooted an eighty-foot
beech tree, sent it crashing
through the roof of our bedroom,
covering us in autumn leaves.

Now, I'm woken by the pigeon
that no longer claps his courtship
from the branch that doesn't rustle
on the tree that isn't there now.

Sometimes I stand at the bus stop,
near the beech tree that isn't there,
listening to the wind that doesn't stir,
waiting for you to arrive on a bus
that doesn't come this way.

Meeting Hitler

36 Crowther Street, Castleford, Yorkshire

Our Mam brought us to Castleford,
some time in nineteen forty-two.
We used the news for tablecloths
and you know what in t'outside loo:
I read of Hitler in East Prussia
and saw a picture of *Wolf's Lair*.
The Fuhrer seemed to stare at me
and snarl as if his teeth were bare.

Mam said Churchill would send him packing.
He allus waved a big cigar,
and made the V for Victory,
his signal that we'd win the war.
That didn't stop my frequent dreams,
when Hitler came to smother me –
I'd wake to find I couldn't move,
till Mam came in and kissed me free.

My Mam called Dr Tome one day:
my squeaky chest was troublin' me.
He said *She needs her tonsils out –
she'll get much stronger then, you'll see.*

Castleford Hospital

Mam brought me here by ambulance
with several other girls and boys,
who seemed to think that this was fun!
You should have heard the bloomin' noise.

They took my clothes. Gave me a robe.
Masked women laid me on a trolley.
Another woman pushed me flat.
I arched my back and hollered *Help me* –
they had a pad of cotton wool
dipped in some foul smelling stuff.
That's when I knew Hitler was there.
It was a trap. I'd play it rough.

The pad was on my mouth. I kicked
and caught the woman quite a smack,
both feet full on. She reeled sideways,
hit the cupboard with her back.
(Churchill would have been so proud of me.)
They rallied, called for help. The door
burst open. A man with fierce blue eyes
glared at me. Hitler – I knew for sure.

The women pushed me, held me down,
one caught my legs, one grabbed an arm.
Hitler took charge. He said *Breathe deep.*
That's it. Let go. Good girl, stay calm.
I felt myself begin to drift –
give in to him, relax, let go.
I sensed the women turn away,
but lay still, so they didn't know
I was awake. Then, monkey quick,

I sat up, spewed out yellow bile –
Hitler's retreat, my all time great –
one last attempt to fly the flag,
short-lived. BLACKOUT ten minutes late.

Teaching Aunt Gwen to Honk

Dover, September 1940

It was scary in the air-raid shelter
listening to bombs explode and shells scream.
Dad said *If you're born to be hung*
you won't drown. But what did that mean?
Great stuff! Mum glared *Three blooming cheers!*
If the shells don't shriek me out, you will.
We might be grounded here for years,
with Grandma's 'Nazi' spit and spat,
her 'what she'd do to Hitler' rabbit,
and these two screeching 'Old MacDonald'
as if their lives depended on it.

Castleford, June 1941

It was safe in Yorkshire. No more bombs
except the ones that Aunt Gwen dropped.
Piglets should be seen, not heard.
Their rowdy honkings must be stopped.
And if they honked another word
they'd end up with their pigtails chopped.

Think kindly Gwen, said Uncle Jack
they'll settle down — it won't take long,
two shell-shocked babbies, far from home
and frightened — let 'em have their song.

So Auntie Gwen, who had no kids,
pinned a smile over looks that kill
and once or twice we heard her snort —
my sister thought her nice until
a sudden wind slammed shut the door
and I screamed like a lunatic
Air-raid, Iris, hit the floor!

Under the table in a flash,
we squashed together like sardines.
I pulled the cloth to hide us, crash
bang wallop fell the china bombs,
exploding into smithereens.
Aunt slapped my leg, I bit her arm,
Iris grabbed her by the legs —
she sprawled into our funny farm —
with a clonk and a honk, honk, honk…

Castleford to Dover, November 1941

Two little piggies turned a page over,
squealing delighted all the way to Dover.

Headstrong

I grabbed my blanket coat and ran
to escape the red-head's temper flashes,
blue-ice warnings and muttered threats,
the wrist-burns and the sudden slaps.
I left her with her fingers trapped,
when the sash-cord on the window snapped.

Safe in the soot-streaked alley
I gambled with my sister's pain –
she'd murder me if she broke loose –
heads I won and tails she lost.
Squatted on an empty coal sack,
I chalked a wild rose on my top
and spun the never-be of my dreams
oblivious to the bully's screams.

Home Front

Ration books. Dried egg. Messerschmitts, and tea-stained legs.
Churchill and Flash Gordon. The wardens doing rounds.
Milk kept cool in bowls of water, scraping marge from home-made bread.
That's how it was.

Neytherum. Turnip pie. Leek and potato pud.
Haricot hotpot. Eggless sponge and carrot cake
swilled down with dandelion and burdock. Digging for victory.
That's how it was.

Pigs' trotters. Scrag-end of neck served with hedgerow pie.
Sausage made of pink breadcrumbs. Raspberry jam with wood-chippings
and how to make the weekend joint last until the next weekend.
That's how it was.

Blackout curtains, two-lump fires and doodlebugs.
Sirens screaming. Hanging round in air-raid shelters.
Dominoes and snakes-and-ladders. Mother shouting *Go to sleep*.
That's how it was.

Learning how to patch a shirt with *Mrs. Sew-and-Sew*.
Make-do-and-mend. Turn your collars and bind your sleeves.
Winter coats from old wool blankets. Cobbled shoes and hand-me-downs.
That's how it was.

No gates. No railings. No aluminium saucepans.
Knitting socks for soldier dads and uncles.
Some would only need one sock, and some would never know the need.

Neytherum. Neither one nor the other: Mother's famous meatless stew.

13

Proper Peaky

From under t'table like a whippet out t'fold,
caught by me knickers like a navvy humping spuds,
She said *By heck lass, tha's proper peaky*.
I said *That's pot callin' t'kettle black*.

Out shot pills like a bullet from a gun.
Up on t'copper like a convict from the hold,
I said *Stuff Dr Williams' pink pills*.
She said *Take yer Dr Williams' pink pills*.

Jumping from t'copper like a monkey from a tree,
kicking like a donkey about to drop its load.
She said *Come on lass, tha's proper peaky*.
I said *That's pot callin' t'kettle black*.

Inta outdoor lavvy like a skiver for a fag,
puffing like a steam train grinding to a halt.
I said *Stuff Dr Williams' pink pills*.
She said *Take yer Dr Pilliams' wink wills*.

Outta lavvy like a savage from the bush,
shiverin' in me shoes like a spook that's got t'flu.
She said *By heck lass, tha's proper peaky*.
I said *That's pot callin' t'kettle black*.

Over t'chair like a fox escapin' t'hounds,
up the 'allway like a thoroughbred colt.
I said *Stuff Dr Williams' pink pills*.
She said *Come on lass, tha's proper peaky*.

Back went me 'ead like a coconut that's floored,
in went t'pills like pebbles in t'pond.
She said *Take yer Dr Pilliams' wink wills.*
I said *Stuff Dr Williams' pink pills.*

Up came me steam like kettle on t'boil,
screaming like a banshee on the razzamatazz.
I said *By heck Mam, tha's proper peaky.*
She said *Stuff Dr Williams' pink pills.*

Caught by her apron strings like a kid playin' hooky,
tied to the doorknob like a mongrel on heat,
she said *By heck lass, A'm proper peaky.*
I said *Take yer Dr Pilliams' wink wills.*

Grandpa's War

The telegram arrived at twelve.

By four-fifteen the concrete yard
had splintered under Grandpa's hammer.
We watched him gather up the pieces,
and stack them in the wheelbarrow.

Mum tried to get the telegram:
Nay lass it's nowt but paper words,
the die is cast, we'll stay our ground,
some things are best digested first.

At six o'clock the job was done,
the rubble cleared, the mangle moved.
We thought he'd stop, come in and rest,
but he had more to do. Much more.

By eight o'clock he'd shaped a garden,
a flowerbed for summer blooms.
We went inside and listened
to the wireless crackling out the news.

At nine he read the telegram:
His eldest, Harry, lost at sea.
We heard him swear beneath his breath,
and whisper — what is, will surely be.

Next day at eight he said *Let's plant*
lavender and lily-of-the-valley.
We chose snapdragons and jam-tarts
and rose bushes for Uncle Harry.

Grandpa wanted fragrant hyacinth
and daffodils – daffodils' yellow lament.
This war is too much black and white –
we need life's beauty, colour, scent.

Dover – 1940

Brave men, made helpless by the storm, fight on
where warring winds write the rubric of battle
and gunmetal seas sound the alert.
Heaving waves ruck and roar, no ease
tonight. *Ida love, your hero has cold feet.*

> *Blast the seas, the sky, the shrunken November sun,*
> *blast the shrieking sound of shells that turns our beaches*
> *to a den of Hell.*

Pier-battery, breakwater submerged
from view; icy torrents pound,
retract their ravenous jaw, then make waterfall
of all. Six shells swept ashore – Death's call is heard
at Knuckle Head – a man we knew. *God spare you*
tonight, Ida.

> Pewter skies glisten in the sleet,
> pale sun splutters, like wet candle tallow. They wrapped him
> in a winding sheet. *Man the pumps, the Eastern Arm is burning*
> *hollow. 'Our days were a joy' Ida ' and our paths through flowers.'*

Shells, shouts, screams. Cordite in the air,
flak, a thousand coloured lights. Blood in hair.
Ida, my love, I smell spring lilac near.
I shall not hear them sound All Clear.

The quoted line in stanza four is from 'After a Journey', by Thomas Hardy.

Corpus Christi

Lying on my back in a field of wheat
watching the world through half-closed lids,
breathing in the patchwork of poppies
pinking the stubble-edged skyline
listening to the faraway sound of people
assembled together for evensong
and the tolling bell that gathers them in
to the high-backed pews of St Paul's
and the cool dimness of the nave,

while I, chaliced in summer gold,
commune with the whispering forest
of wheat, aware of the field mouse balanced
on a well-bent ear, sheen-listening,
watching me watching him harvest:
Pater noster, qui es in coelis.

Tunnel Vision

I wonder what happened to Jimmie,
the braw bandsman, fond of fish and chips,
jive, and gumsucking in the back row,
getting his two and sixpence worth?

Best not talk of it, there's no cure
for the darkness. I know it's wrong,
but if I could be anywhere
I'd be on that God-forsaken bridge,
defying gravity, watching the trains go by,
with Jimmie hanging on to my legs, daring me.

Why Do Fools Fall In Love?
Quite a hit with us in the fifties.
A lot's changed since then, hip-replacements
are common nowadays; you can chase
falling leaves well into your sixties,
turn them over, like crows do,
maybe pick up a plump worm.

I suppose that's what the doctor meant
when he said I'd got tunnel vision.
You'd get more sense from a saxophone.
Oh boy, could Jimmie play one of those.
(Dad said that's where he kept his brains.)
I was putty in his hands.

Nice girls don't canoodle, Mum said.
There's always ignorance and apathy
to stain the snow, like illicit sex
on a white flannelette night-gown.
Best not talk of it, there's no cure
for a clock with a broken spring.

Follow Me

I long to fill her red suede shoes,
to be sixteen, to act grown-up
in stiletto heels with pointed toes
tapping *Follow Me* in heel Morse code.

I envy her those red suede shoes,
their slinky heels, her slim ankles,
the mystique of her female charm
and *Follow Me* of clinking bangles.

I really covet those red suede shoes,
her pointed breasts and scarlet lips,
her green eyeshadow and feline grace,
the *Follow Me* of tiptoe-taps.

I envy her, those red suede shoes,
the blokes she pulls, the furs she wears,
her negligées and silk pyjamas:
the *Follow Me* that whistles wolves.

Convent of the Assumption

Pax vobiscum. My peace I leave with you:
June 1959. The swing of hockey sticks,
stolen strawberries, breaking curfew
to run barefoot across the field to Pegwell Bay. The breadth,
the depth of long untarnished summer days

when stained-glass windows, sapphire, ruby,
sprinkled confetti on oak pews and quiet aisles,
on stately nuns in purple robes,
their timeless faces framed in fluted veils:
the brides of Christ. That heavenly choir,
throbbing through diamond-patterned cloisters.

I was all of fifteen then, a month
or so away from sixteen's agéd wisdom
and Mother Ciaran's whispered myths:
Blessed Virgins and other saintly idioms,
the sanctity of sex and Holy Matrimony
and how to bear the pain with dignity.

Your farmer's hands swinging the thurible,
the way you genuflected
and bowed before the thrice-blessed sacrament.
You trembled as I passed, blushed
as I knelt to relive the ancient mystery,
promise chastity and nightly rosaries.

Those stolen moments in the apple orchards
when the snake appeared and tempted Eve.

The Box Factory

I don't know why I'm here,
dropping this fancy paper on the conveyor belt,
first the left side, then the right, making sure
the glue is evenly spread, before I flip
it over, take a box, centre it, press it down, flip
it towards me, turn it this way,
that way, my fingers deftly folding
the expensive paper, covering the box,
disguising the cheap cardboard,
making it presentable, a saleable commodity,
pink velvet for a single rose, white satin
for a Parker pen.

I don't know why I'm here,
listening to the piped music belting out
Answer Me, Oh My Love, asking myself
what the hell I've done to upset you,
wondering if you'll forgive me,
working faster, fingers automatically
glueing, twisting, turning, covering
the boxes, until they are stacked
in neat rows waiting to be filled.

I don't know why I'm here,
breathing in the God-damned awful
smell of glue rising from the conveyor belts,
praying you still love me,
listening to the empty chatter
of a hundred other factory girls
standing in neat rows preparing, pasting,

covering empty cardboard boxes, slagging
off the bosses, dissecting their latest fling.

I slash cheap lipstick on my dry lips,
clart my face in sun-kissed foundation,
and wonder if my piece-work bonus will stretch
to a white satin Bardot blouse? Something to dress
my wounds, fill me with hope that you
still want to park your pen.

Hearts and Flowers

I've fetched thee here, behind t'bike shed
where there's a pile of new mown hay,
to practise a bit for when we get wed.
I'd not have thee risk a new tool!

Tha mun try it, lass, before thee buy!
Ay mebbe I should, but I'll not!
I'll not walk t'aisle wi' a rabbit in t'pie,
so keep thee mitts under control.

Tha needn't worry, my lass, about that:
this buck's t'smart t'spring thee snare!
Cum nussle close, while I twiddle they twat
and thou feels the goods in my store.

A've told thee to stop, I'm not in t'right mood!
Ey up! Tha deserves to be shot!
How can I tell thee, without being rude,
that there's flowers in t'bloody pot!

Young Mrs Hubbard

Shall I sketch the beech tree today,
charcoal in the shadows round the bark,
or wash the dishes, make the beds,
check the larder, see what's there?

The trunk's divided, split in two,
one faces west, the other south,
like lovers who have grown apart.
He dominates, demands his space,

she stretches forward, reaches further —
the single beds have made themselves.
I'll leave the dishes, let them sink,
the cupboard's bare.

Last Kiss

Who fitted the coin box on your heart,
made you believe you could put a price
on love, as if it can be bought,
with your soul as the auctioneer offering
your loyalties to the highest bidder?

You shook us off like old rags. Sent us
six thousand miles across to Europe —
all those bags, porters, trains, taxis,
hotel meals, with your children's unanswered
questions puzzling my ears, my heart,
and your Judas kiss still throbbing on my cheek.

Afterwards

I took a chisel and attacked the mock pine panelling.
It splintered as I levered it from the living-room walls:
you'd screwed it down tighter than a coffin lid.

Underneath, Jacobean Roses, fawn, embossed in brown
that wouldn't show the dust.
The metal scraper swore across a paper plain.
Did you or I choose the autumn scene,
russet leaves ripped from a naked tree?

What matter?
Drowned under a deluge of warm water
till sodden, it fell facelessly away.

Entombed below, Edwardian Lady,
blue eyebright, sweet mallow, bitter borage,
poppies peopling a wayside.
Tissue thin it clung where it had hung for all those wasted years,

until I, smiling, drew the veil. Water lilies,
suffused in light, petals pinking translucent pools,
illuminating subterranean caverns
where the wild weed grows.

Jackpot

I grabbed the moment, took the money,
chanced the blizzard and fled south,
snowflakes playing noughts and crosses
on the windscreen, eyes chasing the road,
uncertainty, congealed as frozen bone-marrow,
forming glaciers on my inscape,
my entire life flattened, folded
down into a rawhide suitcase, thrown
this way and that as I juggled
with the hairpin bend, crunched to first gear,
scuffed the Metro on a hidden
milestone, cursed my ill luck, drove on
through the ifs and buts of doubt,
cold as the naked sycamore trees marking
the edges of familiar fields, branches
pointing every-which-way, gesticulating
like a tic-tac man lengthening the odds,
irritated by the suitcase banging about,
stacking the deck, shuffling my memories
            me in your favourite mohair sweater,
            you at the greyhound track,
            a pair of unclaimed baby boots,
            dried freesias wrapped in tissue paper,
            a seventy-eight of Frank Sinatra,
            the mortgage arrears I thought you'd paid,
            a betting slip, a Dior dress,
            your forty thousand pounds,
            and a broken string of pearls,
all butting against the back door,

as I clipped the sign, 'Darts Match Cancelled'
outside The Chequers, skidded,
regained control, missed the vicar
struggling uphill, cassock flying out
like a black kite signalling disaster,
clapped bumpers with an abandoned Citroen,
took a glancing blow from the suitcase
as the Metro did an about-turn,
shook me like dice in a metal eggcup,
(this could be a whole new board game)
maybe, just maybe, I can make
it back, open my own bank account,
pay the mortgage, before you wake
with the jackpot headache you were lager-louting
when Lady Luck stacked the odds in my favour —
yes, this is a whole new board game.

Bunny Girl

I keep finding bits of myself
scattered like chewed up paper,
love letters, Dear Johns and so sorrys
alongside the mouse droppings
of earlier lives.

It's a bit like playing finders-keepers
except that sometimes the prize stinks,
stinks of the skeletons buried under
the clean linen of loose covers,
or hidden behind framed photographs
of happy families.

What gets to me most
is the one of a girl frozen in time,
naked, except for a white fur coat,
her woman's eyes startled as a skinned rabbit's,
staring out, waiting for the pot to boil.

Why

The why-child wakes in the cold attic,
where the white moon plays silver tricks
with ferret faces in frosty windows
and burrowing danger scatters fear

over the oak-beamed walls, like flurries
of snow blurring the edge of what is,
until the frozen window-panes
become wet with the ferret's breathings.

The waking nightmare that follows
rips open the white gown of sleep
and the sharp-tooth taste of tomorrow
is the curdled milk of bad dreams.

The why-child is awake in the attic,
afraid of the white daylight moon,
afraid of the ferret familiar
that eats up the long afternoon.

The Big C

She's always there, that younger self,
reminding me that Cleanliness
is next to Godliness – scouring
the stainless steel sink, mindful
of the waste disposal unit, afraid
it might chew a finger, amputate a hand.

She's been cleaning that bloody kitchen
for years, wiping the turquoise fridge,
careful of the catch, mindful of past bruises,
picturing the empty shelves overfull,
real butter, a hunk of Cheddar
and a fridge magnet *I love you.*

She always moves the breadbin, wipes
under it. I can smell the Dettol,
so good for those sudden abrasions.
Her arms are slender, but curvy,
her hair, still damp from the shower
is neatly tied at the base of her neck.

She's always wary, always listening
for his footsteps on the stairs, the hall, and
fearful for herself and for her children.
They must not be sullied by the filth
who wrapped his fingers in her pony tail and …

Second Thoughts

I've taken the advice of counsellors,
hoping we might salvage something,
a glass of wine, a verse of poetry?
But no, we've nothing in common,
we should have parted years ago,
before this strange attachment grew.

I've locked the door on our well-wishers,
tried hard to accept the isolation
of being on my own with you
always there, in my head, pressing on me,
stealing my time, cramping my space.

It's too late now to cut you out,
you've filled me with your unwanted self.
Your tentacles are too widely spread,
Mr Carcinoma in my head.

Cutting Back the Delphiniums

The delphiniums are fierce this year,
thunderous purple, ragged from the storm;
their waywardness spikes your crown of thorns,
fuels your hidden agenda,
the piled-up grievances that chip mugs,
or break a favourite vase.
My cue to exit, leave the room,
the house, put a measure of space

between us. Recall the delphiniums'
unruly victory and my creative clutter:
sketch books, pencils, watercolours,
patchwork squares and knitting patterns,
the homely things you call a criminal
waste of space. Time to decide whether
to accept your over-zealous pruning
or scatter seed on more fertile ground.

Make Do and Mend

Why did you leave me your dressmaking patterns?
You were the seamstress. I can't sew.
I can't make something out of nothing. Even if
I could unpick my life, I couldn't re-stitch it.

I'm not home-making material. I'd fray
at the edges. Let's face it, Cynthia,
your favourite A-line, with the long sleeves
and round neckline, cut well below
the calves, would smother me.

The flaws in the cloth would show. I'm not
your washable, crease resistant, any temperature,
prefer to be tumble-dried sort of a woman.
I'd shrink if I tried to live up to you.

Growing Familiar

There's a deceit in familiar things,
the old settee, the scratched piano,
the teapot in its striped waistcoat,
and your face over morning coffee

scrunched up like the faded tissue paper
in that box in the attic,
the one you've kept locked for over
forty years and want me to burn

before I find out for myself
something I've known almost as long
as you and never spoken of,
something I wish you'd shared with me
before the petals of your face
faded into crumpled tissue.

Is it too late to sling the teapot,
buy a new settee, tell you I know
I'm not his father, but love
fleshes out skin and bone?

Branching Out

The cherry tree centres the garden. Its shade
reaches out, touches your vacant chair,
sneaks in through the bay window, flecking
the piano. I lift the lid, finger the ivory keys,
touch middle C and suddenly it's Chopin,
sadly-hopeful, tender-true: a prelude
to low-key my grief. The sun steeples,
fills the room. Its warmth relaxes me,

and in this altered state I feel you near,
hear you call my name, watch you pattern
and re-pattern sun-specks of household dust
into a consonance of light and shade,
a gentle nocturne from the shadowlands.
There's a butterfly in the cherry tree.

Bitter-sweet

Yes, I still play our tune. The quick, quick, slow
of *Love and Marriage*, glib and sweetly trite
and your receding footprints in the snow,

and how I pleaded with you, please don't go.
My words were rainbows, yours were black and white.
Yes, I still play our tune. The quick, quick, slow

of one last kiss before your final no,
and how I trembled, though my smile was bright –
and your receding footprints in the snow.

The loss, the emptiness, the body-blow
that left me weak, a shaken thing, no fight.
Yes, I still play our tune, the quick, quick, slow

of it. The tummy gripes of told you so,
no sparklers, no Catherine-wheels that night,
just your receding footprints in the snow.

I got your letter, bitter-sweet as sloe
gin, bottled in summer, sipped by firelight.
Yes I still play our tune: the quick, quick, slow
of your receding footprints in the snow.

Antique Lace

Settee and armchairs with antimacassars,
silk flowers in vases standing tall, casting
strange shadows on high-ceilinged walls.

See how slowly stiffened fingers crawl
across the broad expanse of crochet shawl,
counting double-trebles, teasing out the fringe.

Blind-eyed she sights herself

barefoot on wet sands, scaling loose slack
to the tumbledown shack where they lay
in love long gone...

See how she wrestles, pulls it sideways,
finds remembered corals, carmine red that streaks
the blue, as when the sun shuts down the day.

Blind-eyed she finds and feels its edges –
digs her bony fingers through the damaged loops,
as if to catch and tie each broken thread:

scratch of sea-birds' claws
on the corrugated roof augurs
ebb tide: fields choreographed in green
give way to mists, somnolent grey,
soft-focused now as evensong...

Settee and armchairs with antimacassars,
silk flowers in vases standing tall, casting
strange shadows on high-ceilinged walls.

The Listener

You mustn't get so low, ring me instead!
You know my number, yet you never phone.
Most illness, don't forget, is in the head,
so why sit moping here? And all alone.

You need a friend, someone to cheer you up,
someone to trust and tell your troubles to.
I'll step in when I can, to take a cup
of tea and be a listening ear for you.

I'm sorry, dear, but soon I'll have to dash,
I've got so many things to do, laundry
and dinner to prepare, a cheque to cash.
Heavens! I've missed the bank. My memory

is over-loaded! Ah! I see you read,
how nice to have the time. I used to once,
but now I fear my mind has run to seed.
I'm sure you've got me down as quite a dunce.

But there! A mother's always on the trot!
So think of me, while you're just sitting here,
be grateful for the hours that you've got
to spend on pleasant things in life. My dear,

I see you draw. And you are quite a painter.
I'm sure it must be good for you to try.
Not bad, my dear, but make your colours fainter,
your yellow's harsh against that pallid sky.

I must be off now or I'll miss my bus,
my old head aches with all your lively chatter.
Goodbye! God bless! You really mustn't fuss.
I'll come back soon, I know you love to natter.

You mustn't cry... I've said I'll come again!
We'll say a little prayer before I go
to thank the Lord you're not in any pain.
Eyes closed, please listen while I tell Him so!

Sestina

It doesn't matter how you tell the story,
as long as you remember how it starts:
the sun must fizzle out in darkened skies
and furtive shadows creep across the lawn.
Of course there is a churchyard and a ghost,
and usually a child who's lost his way.

A frightened child who always asks the way,
and finds himself mixed up in someone's story —
something about a churchyard and a ghost
who makes his presence felt in fits and starts
before his furtive walk across the lawn
to leave his shadowed outline on the skies.

Next day beneath the ever-blue of skies
the tale seems set to move a different way:
afternoon tea served on a sunlit lawn
is more in keeping with a shared love story,
one that finishes where tender kisses start
and no-one stops to think they've seen a ghost

until the heroine disturbs that ghost
whose phantom fingers creep across the skies
and rushes back to where the story starts
to try and make it end a different way.
The problem is you have to start the story
where furtive shadows creep across the lawn

and once those shadows creep across the lawn
it's almost certain that you'll see the ghost

and set the wheels in motion for a story
where sunlight fizzles out in darkened skies.
There doesn't seem to be another way,
 the end is anchored where the story starts —

the curtains rise, the cast appears: it starts
as scary shadows slant the haunted lawn —
the child who's lost won't go a different way,
he'll stumble in alone, afraid. The ghost
will rise, disturb the sun and blacken skies,
he's present now and always, it's his story

and, like all stories, it must end. And start —
it's happening now — the troubled sky, the lawn,
the ghost await the child who's lost his way...

Backside Up

I'm a side-out, side-in, side-down, ward-up
meet myself turning-re wards-back,
ears in armpits, teeth in nostrils,
eyes in earholes, past my by-sell
tidy-un, patient-im, hardy-fool
boy who never goes to school.

I'm pudent-im , a noxious-ob,
a cal-ras, wag-scally, ward-awk yob,
a crack shot with an apult-cat
an obrill, perb-su, board-skate do-kid,
my Mam's up-fed, me dad's out fagged,
I'll him dodge fore-be get I a clout,
too late, found I, dad mine's no fool,
he's kicked my side-back off to school.

Artistic Licence

I know you need a holiday, my dear,
we'll take a cottage in the weald of Kent;
I've promised you a break, we'll go in June.
I've seen a lovely place that's up for rent.

The toilet's out of doors, a hundred yards
or so. The views will drive you frantic.
No running water. No electric. But
mellow candlelight is so romantic.

I'll paint all day so you can sit and rest.
No, no my dear, there are no shops nearby
but you can cook, I know you'll love it so,
the oil stove is quite rustic. Time will fly.

We'll soon be there. The air will do you good,
the village store has all the food we'll need.
The walk will bring you back to health. You'll see,
we'll wish the strain upon your face, Godspeed.

Six weeks of bliss! Make sure you pack my paints.
I'll capture you sweet as a ripened plum,
washing our clothes in the chalk-hewn stream —
a masterpiece to frame for years to come.

Limbo

When sea-mists make life hell for motorists
and foghorns haunt the becalmed straits
and cliff-top-silence stifles peace,
your skeleton sings *We'll meet again*.
Then all unrhymed and yellowed thoughts
stretch naked on black-satin sheets,
like sour breath and marigold,
or bitter almonds in mulled wine.

The melting down of stolen gold,
the crucifix that has no clasp,
the unscrewed scream from china jars,
the locket with no photograph,
tears and pearls in a leitmotif,
a bridal veil drawn down on grief.

Consider the Lily

                              Can you explain
the silver sound of midnight waves,
the almond taste of joy and pain,
the candlelight that warms cool caves?

The silver sound of midnight waves
adds honeydew to chocolate bars.
The candlelight that perfumes caves
ignites a galaxy of stars,

adds honeydew to chocolate bars.
A twist of lime, a hint of peach
ignites a galaxy of stars:
one bride, one groom, one ring, one chapel,

a twist of lime, a hint of peach,
the almond taste of joy and pain,
one life, one love incense the chapel.

David's God

My grandson David's almost five,
he's serious with large grey eyes
that question everything he sees.
Yesterday, he told me God was blue,
and sometimes red and yellow too,
but never green.

He told me how, on Bomb-fire night,
when God was black he'd heard the BANG
of fireworks. And how great FIREBALLS
had burned the sky. He thought bad men
had murdered God. It made him cry.

It made him think. He asked
if leaves would grow again on trees,
and new life come to burnt-out grass?
And later on, if God is green.

Windings

I heard the rumba of the rain,
saw steam rise up from tarmac roads,
blue flax unbutton flower-heads
and poppies burst to ragbag reds.

I heard the whispered threat in winds
that whistled through the flowering weeds,
disturbing heavy-headed docks
unsettling dandelion clocks.

I heard the tractor's warning roar
as cutters sliced through waiting corn,
the plastic shroud drawn in at lips
and snap of metal binding clips:

an airless moment, edgy, tense,
auguring certainty's silence.

Pining

(for Janet Bailey)

I don't mind the walk, but I miss you;
it's lonely crossing unploughed fields.
There's a rough path that bears westwards
towards a line of chalk-warped firs –
Picasso cut in blue.

I found a path on the other side,
a straight mile, arrow-straight;
it runs across the downs, then disappears
into sunset. The Romans built it about 50 AD.
They say, when moonlight and ebb-tide meet
you can hear them marching.

I'm sitting here now, on a fallen pine,
taking a breather, so to speak,
listening to seagulls a couple of fields
back, airborne behind a tractor,
envying their unison of silver,
their squawk of survival.

Did you know there are violets,
huge patches under the hedgerow,
as if there'd been a skyslide?
If you sit next to me on the pine
I'll show you. And maybe, just maybe,
we'll meet in the blues.

Cold October

(for Jan and John Hughes)

Off-stage, enjoying wine, two lovers sit.
Although they've heard the bell for curtain call,
they steal a second more and polish it,
then rise to play their part and give their all.

Sauntering down la Place de la Concorde,
a dream they've shared through all their married years,
he buys her things she knows he can't afford,
her love for him holds back the ready tears.

He hides his tiredness by talk, but she
sees all: the dragging feet that strive and climb,
the way he holds her hand so tenderly,
then softly lets it slide. How brief is time.

The script's all wrong, but who's to tell? Or know
they laugh when they should cry? She plays her part
until the final act when he must go,
then finds the words burst out from her full heart.

The bitter sweetness of those final days
distilled by her, by him forever lost,
embalms the memories she now replays
as cold October turns to winter frost.

Gathering Lilac

She was always going somewhere...

Those last five years she died with me
were spent in gathering lilac.
I don't know who you are my dear,
but thanks a lot. How kind you've been.
I hope we'll meet again quite soon.
Then I'd be Mum and hold her tight,
and beg her stay a little while,
remind her how we used to sing
We'll Gather Lilac in the Spring.

She was always going somewhere...

Those last five years she died with me
were spent in gathering lilac.
A policeman brought her back one day,
a naked mouse in an overcoat;
she spat and screamed and scratched at me
as if I'd sprung the trap that nailed her.
I took her by the hand and sang
the words she knew and loved so well,
she held me close, my Mum, until —

she was always going somewhere...

Those last five years she died with me
were spent in gathering lilac.
She'd pack her handbag furtively,
a comb, a photograph of Dad,

a twig cut from the lilac tree.
Put out the light! The warden's here!
Your father's legs are weeping shrapnel.

She was always going somewhere,
those last five years she died with me.
I don't know who you are my dear
but thanks a lot. How kind you've been.
I said *Goodnight, God bless you Mum.*
We'll Gather Lilac in the Spring.

Attar of Grandmama

Memories locked in a cedarwood box:
attar of Grandmama lingering on.

Sun through her windows warming the pots,
ashes of violets, mercerised wax,
gardenia talc to sprinkle her stays,
rosewater tissue and lavender bags.

Straighten the bedclothes, fragrant of her.
Remember the nights that I nestled in there
her arms warm around me, the perfume she wore,
the powder pomander hung on the door.

Bathe her body in lavender oil,
dabble her temples with eau-de-cologne,
kiss the last words from her fast-cooling lips,
tidy the bottles and screw down the lids.

Mirror, Mirror

(for my sister, Iris)

You were proud of that polka-dot dress,
the yellow one I watched you cut, pin, tack
and sew on Granny's treadle –
the old Singer I turned butter on
once, when Mam wanted me quiet.

Gran said you'd done a perfect job.
I didn't like the colour much,
it reminded me of Colman's Mustard,
but it leapt off you like gold coins
from a spendthrift, set light to your hair.

I saw you framed in Grandad's mirror,
you looked different, more grown-up.
I knew there'd be no more hopscotch
or me chanting *Rain, rain, go away*
while you skipped *another washing day*.

Something in me snapped: I ripped your strap
spat tin-tacks and razor blades.
You called me cow, and jealous pig.
You weren't to know that I had heard
the Shepherd calling in his sheep.

I watched you bend towards yourself
like Eve discovering the first woman
in the pine-edged glass of Grandad's mirror,
your skin grown pale as arum lilies,
the organ playing *Abide With Me*.

Dear Iris

(for my sister Iris who died of a brain tumour, aged 42)

I've still got the rose you gave me,
pressed in the Family Bible,
its petals, once perfect pink, faded
thin and dry as old paper.

The doubts set in two days before
you died, I was okay till then,
sure I'd done my best to shield you,
to give you hope when all seemed lost;

but when you crammed the lime ice-lolly
between your dry and swollen lips
and it met the bars of your clamped teeth,
I knew you'd lost the means of speech.

I wish I hadn't lied to you,
made believe that you'd get well,
swim, dance, go back to work,
be there for Cheryl, Anne and Kevin.

I should have halved your painful path,
you showed me clearly that you knew,
but I ignored your openings,
forced you to face your death alone.

I felt myself get up to run,
to leave behind the smell of blood
but I (the liar, coward, thief) turned
to face the *mea culpa* of my grief.

I held your quiet hands in mine,
made promises, I knew I'd keep,
into your unresponsive ears
till you, blind-eyed, were lost to tears.

o o o

Yea, though I walk through the valley of the shadow of death,
I will fear no evil: for thou art with me;
thy rod and thy staff they comfort me.

There was no kindly shepherd,
only Father Fahey on automatic pilot,
issuing countless farewells to Iris,
begging us to pray for your departed

soul as if you'd gone by train
and we should stand and wave goodbye!
His words set Dad's frantic arms around
my neck. He squeezed me dry.

I remembered your clamped teeth,
the way you looked in death
and found no comfort in the psalms,
no belief in resurrection.

Dad's tears were on my face and neck,
his pleadings in my ears. And so we stayed
until the organ played the final dirge,
and you were carried to the hearse.

o o o

The afternoon was wet.
A strike at Dover docks had stopped
the traffic. Freight lorries, transit vans, caravans and campers

all stood still.

While you, cradled in the procession of life,
slept on, oblivious to the honking horns,
the panic and the pandemonium. We were
behind the hearse, aware of the mounting anger,

the sweating streets, the leaden skies,
the muted monotone of falling rain,
the rebellious cursing of irate men;
and the mourners dressed in black.

They let you through. We watched you go,
pell mell towards the crematorium,
while we were powerless to move,
as in a photograph that said it all.

Latintudes

I'm sick of high-faluting platitudes
from they-who-walk-the-water Holy Joes
whose pulpit voices shout our do-si-dos.
Such cloudy silver-lined Beatitudes
and narrow lane no turning attitudes
proportion them the highs and us the lows.
I've had my fill of Punch and Judy shows,
the frenzied zeal of moral rectitudes.

There's life beyond the tudes of Lat and Long,
unnetted seas where men have pearls for eyes,
where love comes first and all feel they belong
and no one needs to question their cap size.
No carrion crows to double-talk plainsong,
or leach the scarlet dawn of clouded whys.

Fair Isle

Assemble all the skeins in readiness,
the pattern has begun; weave in charcoal
and feather stitch cerise, let warmth redress
the sombre morning tones. Reverse the role

of black by weaving it behind the red
of early sky. Increase the opal grey
of clouds and work intarsia. Now shred
with silver strands – slip one – to sun-slit day.

Unravel gold and work in cable stitch
between the loops of lapis blue. Make fast.
The pattern is complete. Sun rays enrich
the Fair Isled dawn of day. It's time to cast

                                        off black.